MW01052730

Citizenship

By Bruce S. Glassman

With an Introduction by
Michael Josephson,
Founder of CHARACTER COUNTS!SM

JOSEPHSON
INSTITUTE
CHARACTERCOUNTS!

Produced and created in partnership with Josephson Institute

Special Thanks goes to the following people, whose help on this project was invaluable:

At CHARACTER COUNTS!:
Michael Josephson
Rich Jarc
Amanda Skinner
Mimi Drop
Michelle Del Castillo

Content Advisers:
Dave Bender, book publisher
Tracy Hughes, educator
& CHARACTER COUNTS!
coordinator for Meadowbrook
Middle School, San Diego
Cindy De Clercq, Elementary
School Principal

And thanks to:
Nathan Glassman-Hughes,
Emma Glassman-Hughes,
Natalia Mata, Erica Warren,
Ebony Sanders, Kellen
O'Connell, Nicole Rigler,
and Alex Olberding

Library of Congress Cataloging-in-Publication Data

Glassman, Bruce.
Citizenship / written by Bruce S. Glassman. — 1st ed.
p. cm. — (Six Pillars of Character series)
Includes bibliographical references and index.
ISBN-13: 978-1-60108-502-3 (hardcover); ISBN-10: 1-60108-502-8 (hardcover)
ISBN-13: 978-1-60108-503-0 (pbk.); ISBN-10: 1-60108-503-6 (pbk.)
1. Citizenship—Juvenile literature. I. Title.

JK1759.G52 2009
323.6—dc22   2008001185
Printed in China

Contents

Thinking About Character

By Michael Josephson, Founder, CHARACTER COUNTS!

Imagine that you're taking a big test at the end of the year. You really want to do well on it. You're stuck on a few questions—answers you know will make the difference between a good grade and a possible poor grade. You look up from your test and realize that you can clearly read the answers from the student sitting next to you. You're now faced with a choice. Do you copy the answers or do you go back to staring at your own sheet?

You consider the choices. You know that, if you cheat, you probably won't get caught. And, you think to yourself, copying a few answers is relatively harmless. Who does it hurt? And, besides, everyone does it, right?

Every day you are faced with choices that test your character.

So, what do you do?

Your honest answer to this question will tell you a great deal about your character. Your answer reflects not only what you know is right and wrong, but also how you *act* with what you know.

You are faced with important choices every day. Some choices are "preference choices"—for example, what to wear to school, what to buy for lunch, or what to buy your dad for his birthday. Other choices are "ethical choices." These choices are about what's right and wrong. These are the choices that reflect character.

Ethics play a part in more daily decisions than you may think. The test-taking scenario is only one example of an ethical choice.

You are faced with ethical choices every day. One of the main goals of this series is to show you how to recognize which choices are ethical choices. Another main goal is to show you how to make the right ethical choices.

About Being Ethical

Being ethical isn't simply about what is allowed—or legal—and what is not. You can often find a legal way to do what is unethical. Maybe you saw that a cashier at the grocery store forgot to ring up one of your items. There is no law that says you must tell him or her. But, is it ethical to just walk out without mentioning it? The answer is no. You're still being dishonest by taking something you did not pay for.

So, being ethical is about something more than "what you can get away with." It is about what you do because *you know it's the right thing to do*—regardless of who's watching and regardless of whether you may stand to gain. Often there is a price to pay for doing the right thing.

Character Takes Courage

There are many obstacles to being ethical—chances are you're faced with some of them every day. Maybe you don't want to be

There are many obstacles to being ethical. Overcoming them takes courage and hard work.

embarrassed by telling the truth. Or maybe you feel doing the right thing will take too much effort. Few good things come without a cost. Becoming a person of character is hard work. Here is a poem I wrote that makes this point.

It's Not Easy

Let's be honest. Ethics is not for wimps.

It's not easy being a good person.

It's not easy to be honest when it might be costly, to play fair when others cheat or to keep inconvenient promises.

It's not easy to stand up for our beliefs and still respect differing viewpoints.

It's not easy to control powerful impulses, to be accountable for our attitudes and actions, to tackle unpleasant tasks or to sacrifice the now for later.

It's not easy to bear criticism and learn from it without getting angry, to take advice or to admit error.

It's not easy to really feel genuine remorse and apologize sincerely, or to accept an apology graciously and truly forgive.

It's not easy to stop feeling like a victim, to resist cynicism and to make the best of every situation.

It's not easy to be consistently kind, to think of others first, to judge generously, to give the benefit of the doubt.

It's not easy to be grateful or to give without concern for reward or gratitude.

It's not easy to fail and still keep trying, to learn from failure, to risk failing again, to start over, to lose with grace or to be glad for the success of another.

It's not easy to avoid excuses and rationalizations or to resist temptations.

No, being a person of character is not easy.

That's why it's such a lofty goal and an admirable achievement.

Character Is Worth It!

I sincerely hope that you will learn and use the ideas of CHARACTER COUNTS! The books in this series will show you the core values (the Six Pillars) of good character. These values will help you in all aspects of your life—and for many years to come. I encourage you to use these ideas as a kind of "guide-rail" on your journey to adulthood. With "guide-rails," your journey is more likely to bring you to a place where you can be a truly good, happy, and ethical person.

Michael Josephson
Founder of Josephson Institute and CHARACTER COUNTS!

chapter 1

What Is Citizenship?

Y ou may think the term *citizenship* is just about an immigrant becoming a citizen of a country. But citizenship has a broader meaning. It means being a responsible member of a community or society.

In most societies, there are expectations of each individual member. Citizens are expected to perform certain duties—such as serving on a jury. They are also expected to exercise certain rights—such as the right to vote. Citizens are also expected to conduct themselves responsibly, to obey the law, and to behave in a way that respects the rights of others.

Good citizens become involved in the issues that affect their government.

If you think about it, being a good citizen—a good member of a community—applies to many parts of your life. You are a member of many different communities at the same time. As a human being on this earth, you are a "citizen of the world," a member of the world community. As an American or a Canadian, for example, you are a member of a national community. On a smaller scale, you are also a member of your neighborhood community, your school community, and maybe an ethnic, religious, or hobby-based community. And, last but not least, you are a member of your family community.

So, what does it mean to be a good member of a community? In general, there are four ingredients to being a good citizen:

1. Fulfilling your civic duties
2. Doing your share
3. Pursuing civic virtues and noble efforts
4. Respecting Authority

Let's look at each of these things more closely.

Your family is one community in which you are a member.

Fulfilling Your Civic Duties

In order for a society to function properly there must be expectations of behavior for every individual. The same is true for any organized group of people—each person must "do their part" to make the whole a success.

Different societies are founded on different principles. Some are democracies, and some are not. In a democracy, individuals are expected to participate in making the democracy function. They do that by voting, voicing their opinions, paying taxes, and serving in the justice system on a jury.

Serving on a jury is one way that people fulfill their civic duty.

Members in a democracy are also expected to do their civic duty by reporting crimes, or taking action to prevent or stop crimes. They are also expected to serve as witnesses if necessary. Some people are afraid to "get involved" if they see a crime happen. Others think "someone else" will surely help or get involved in a crisis if they don't. But what happens when everyone in a society waits for someone else to take action?

Consider this story about taking action:

Late in the middle of the night, a loud fire alarm began to blare in the neighborhood of Creekview Terrace. The alarm did its job well. It was so loud, that it woke residents a few blocks away in every direction.

In one house, the people decided to wait and see if the alarm would stop after a few minutes. "These things are mostly false alarms," they said to each other.

In another house, the kids came running into their parents' bedroom. The parents comforted the kids by saying, "Don't worry. That alarm is so loud, I'm sure someone has already called the fire department."

In still another house, the people remarked that "most fire alarms" are wired directly to fire stations, so the fire department is probably already on its way."

But the alarm did not stop blaring. After ten minutes, another family looked out its living room window and saw the orange glow of flames in the darkness. When they saw that, they said to each other, "Now I'm sure someone called the fire department. You can see the flames!"

Another ten minutes went by. The people of Creekview Terrace were now starting to worry. The alarm had been blasting for more than twenty minutes and there was no sound of fire engines, no horns blaring, no lights flashing.

Slowly, a number of residents made their way out of their homes and walked toward the burning house. As they collected in the street, each asked the other if someone had called the fire department. No one had.

Finally, the fire engines arrived. When they pulled up to the fire, they saw that the house was already lost. Flames had consumed the entire home within the first twenty minutes. If someone had called when the alarm first went off, there would have been time to save it. But no one had. Everyone in Creekview Terrace assumed that someone else had already called.

This example may seem farfetched, but it is not. Countless crimes and tragedies have taken place because people have been unwilling to speak up or take action.

Citizens have a civic duty to take responsibility for their own actions as well. If, for example, you accidently crash your bike into someone's car and scratch it, you have a civic responsibility to report the accident to the owner and help to fix it. Your civic duty also extends to protecting the environment around you. Good citizens are not wasteful, do not pollute, and clean up after themselves.

Doing Your Share

Good citizenship is an important part of good character. It is a

way to think of others instead of only yourself. Acts of good citizenship are acts that benefit other people or the functioning of a community. They are acts that are not done to benefit you directly. They are things that are done because they are good and helpful to all concerned.

Protecting the environment is a big part of civic duty.

Being a good citizen is also about working for what is called "the common good." The "common good" has to do with things that better the world at large. You can work for the common good by helping your school, your neighborhood, or by volunteering at a big organization. The point of working for the common good is to take action that benefits others on a larger scale.

One action to benefit the "common good" is recycling.

Pursuing Civic Virtues and Noble Efforts

As you have read, taking action is a key to being a good citizen. Some action is expected of each person, such as voting. But other actions, though not required, are admirable and strengthen character. We call these things "civic virtues." Civic virtues include running for an elected office, or accepting an appointment to take responsibility for some common effort.

Another example of civic virtue is giving time and/or money to support charitable causes or important issues and beliefs. This is one of many areas where the character pillars of caring, responsibility, and citizenship overlap. Helping to strengthen causes you believe in is at the very heart of being a good citizen.

The Importance of Voting

Electing the president of the United States is one of the most important things America does as a nation. So, would you be surprised to learn that barely half of all eligible voters actually vote in presidential elections?

It's true. In the 2004 election, 55.3% of all eligible voters went to the polls. In 2000, the turnout was 51.3%. And, believe it or not, the presidential election in 1996 only got 49.1% of the voters to cast their ballots. That means the majority of America's voters stayed home!

The statistics for voter turnout in mid-term elections is even worse. (Mid-term elections happen in between presidential elections—in the "off years.") In 2002, for example, only 37% of eligible voters went to the polls. The presidency was not being decided, but seats in the Senate and the House of Representatives were being filled. In fact, turnout for mid-term elections hasn't been more than 40% since 1970. That's almost 40 years ago!

So, why are Americans so bad at participating in the voting process? There are many opinions. One of the most widely accepted is called "voter apathy," which means many people simply don't care to be part of the process. Apathy is often caused by young voters feeling that—whether they vote or don't—"nothing will change." One researcher, Curtis Gans, says that young people also increasingly have a feeling that

The CNN/YouTube presidential debate

"their vote doesn't matter."

Some efforts in recent years have made a difference with young voters. A web site called "Rock the Vote" works to fight censorship, and promotes civic activity by offering voter registration, discussion boards, and activism links. In the past, MTV has sponsored a campaign called "Choose or Lose," which introduces issues and covers campaigns specifically from a young person's perspective.

The growth of the Internet has also increased participation. In 2007 and 2008, the public was able to ask presidential candidates questions directly through YouTube. The responses were televised on CNN.

How can you help to strengthen voter turnout? The first thing is: make sure you participate in school and community elections and debates. The second thing: encourage your friends to get involved, too.

Respecting Authority

A democracy cannot work unless most of its members agree to be governed by laws. The laws to which we agree may change over time, but the fundamental idea remains: society is organized around laws. The laws that form the foundation of everything we do were laid out in our Constitution.

Respecting laws is a key part of being a good citizen. And so is respecting the authority we give to people that help to run our society.

Almost everyone in our society has some kind of authority. Parents in a family have authority. Teachers in your school have authority. Umpires at a Little League game have authority. Elected officials in your town have authority. The President of the United States has authority.

For a society to work properly, members must respect the authority that is given to certain people. It must be an understanding that is shared by all. Think of it as a solid double-yellow line running down the middle of a road. There is nothing that physically stops you from driving over it, but the shared understanding among all lawful drivers is that this kind of line is not to be crossed. Authority is the same way. People agree to live by shared rules and to give certain people the power to make certain decisions. The authority we place in people helps us organize our society. And being organized is important to functioning properly.

Does this mean you should never question authority? No. Authority is only as good as the character of the person who has it. Some people abuse their authority. Others have poor judgment. Challenging authority that is being used unjustly is as important as respecting authority that is fair.

The Basis of Civil Disobedience

Respect for the law is one of the foundations upon which a society is built. But, just because something is a law, does not mean it is right. Civil disobedience is about fighting unjust laws or authority in a way that respects the laws as a whole.

Nonviolent protests are one of the most common forms of civil disobedience. Speaking out against injustice is not only a right in a democracy, it is also a necessity.

Do you know of policies or rules that are unfair or unjust? If so, what can you do to help change them? How many peaceful, nonviolent ways can you think of to make a difference or create a change?

Throughout our history, many unjust laws have been changed by civil disobedience. These acts of protest may have seemed hurtful or "Anti-American" in their time, but they ultimately made America a stronger and fairer nation. We will look at civil disobedience in more detail in the chapter that follows.

The Supreme Court has changed many laws that were proven to be unjust.

chapter 2

The Importance of Citizenship

When you look back in history, you can see that not all societies have been based on just laws. As you know, citizenship is about being involved in a community or society. A good citizen is involved in supporting all that is good, but also in changing what is bad. A truly good citizen does whatever is possible to make sure everyone enjoys the benefits of respect, caring, and fairness. It is no accident that those are also three of the Pillars of Character.

Martin Luther King, Jr. (left) led the fight for civil rights and equality in the 1960s. >

Sam Adams

In every era of history, there have been people who have stood up to injustice. Some have succeeded. Many have failed. In some cases, people have confronted injustice with force. Other times, violence has erupted from protests or resistence that began peacefully.

In Colonial America, for example—just before the Revolution—the colonists organized boycotts of British goods to protest unfair taxes. Other forms of protest followed. The famous Boston Tea Party of 1773—organized by Samuel Adams and others—took the protests to another level. On that occasion, colonists dumped crates of British tea into the harbor, destroying a large amount of valuable cargo. It was not long before British troops were ordered to take up arms against the colonists. For nearly three years, the British and the colonists were at war. Thousands died, but in the end, the colonists had won their independence.

Peaceful Protest

In an open and democratic society, positive change should happen without violence. In America, for example, the Founders who wrote the Constitution put guarantees for individual rights in the Bill of Rights (the first ten amendments to the Constitution). The very first amendment in the Bill of Rights says:

The U.S. Constitution ensures all people the right to protest injustice.

> *Congress shall make no law respecting an establishment of religion, or prohibiting the free exercise thereof; or abridging the freedom of speech, or of the press; or the right of the people peaceably to assemble, and to petition the government for a redress of grievances.*

This Amendment establishes a clear process by which citizens of a free society can work to change injustice. The last phrase specifically grants citizens the right to assemble peacefully in protest and to demand change from their government.

Women's Suffrage and Slavery

In the 1700s and 1800s, slavery was legal in America. During that era, neither slaves nor women had the right to vote. In fact, slaves and women were restricted from many things under the law. Though white women did not suffer the physical hardships that slaves did, slaves and women were both regarded as "second class citizens."

In the 1820s, a woman writer named Fanny Wright started a movement to abolish slavery and give women the right to vote. For nearly 20 years, Wright found little support for her ideas. It wasn't until 1840 that two other women joined her cause. By 1848, Lucretia Mott and Elizabeth Cady Stanton had organized the Women's Rights Convention at Seneca Falls, New York. The convention's resolution said it was "the duty of all women of this country to secure to themselves the sacred right to the elective franchise [the right to vote]."

Fanny Wright (above left), Lucretia Mott (above center), and Susan B. Anthony (above right).

Women protested peacefully for nearly a hundred years before winning the right to vote.

The Civil War ended in 1865, and one year later Stanton and Mott were joined by Susan B. Anthony and Lucy Stone. Together, the four women established the American Equal Rights Association. Their main mission was to secure voting rights for women and African-Americans. They staged protests in cities—primarily along the East Coast—and published literature that promoted their cause.

In 1869, Stanton and Anthony formed a new organization called The National Woman Suffrage Association. This organization criticized the Fourteenth and Fifteenth Amendments to the Constitution, which gave African-Americans greater rights, but still prohibited women from voting.

In 1913, a woman's rights activist named Alice Paul joined with Lucy Burns and Olympia Brown to create the Women's Social and Political Union. These women used more dramatic methods to get their voices heard. They organized huge demonstrations all over the country. They picketed at the White House every day. Over the next few years, more than 500 women protestors were arrested, and 168 were jailed. Alice Paul was sentenced to seven months in prison.

President Woodrow Wilson announced in 1918 that giving women the vote was "urgently needed." Although the House of Representatives passed a women's suffrage amendment, the Senate defeated it. It wasn't until May of 1919 that both houses of Congress finally passed an amendment that gave women voting rights. In 1920, the Nineteenth Amendment officially became law.

Henry David Thoreau

It had taken about 100 years, but the women's suffrage movement finally achieved its goal—and without violence. Starting in the 1860s, the use of nonviolent protest came to be known as "civil disobedience." The term—and many of the ideas behind it—came from the writings of a man named Henry David Thoreau.

In 1848, Thoreau gave a lecture entitled "The Rights and Duties of the Individual in Relation to Government." The ideas he expressed soon developed

Henry David Thoreau

into an essay called "Resistence to Civil Government."

Thoreau likened government to a big machine. He said that when the machine was producing injustice, it was the civic duty of its citizens to be a "counter friction"—in other words: to provide resistance. Thoreau also believed that, in a democracy, majorities are not necessarily wise and just. He argued that—just because a majority believes or supports something—does not make it right. Slavery, which was legal in Thoreau's time, was a perfect example of that fact.

Martin Luther King, Jr. was greatly influenced by the writings of Henry David Thoreau.

Thoreau also said "you serve your country poorly if you do so by suppressing your conscience in favor of the law." What did he mean? He did not mean that citizens should necessarily break the law. But he was saying that laws are sometimes unjust, and the citizen who works to change them is doing his or her country the greatest possible service.

Thoreau's ideas about government and society continued to gain popularity and acceptance, even after he died in 1862. In 1866, a collection of Thoreau's work was published under the now famous title "Civil Disobedience."

The Great Influence of Civil Disobedience

In the early 1900s, Mohandas Gandhi led India to its independence from Britain. As the leader of the struggle, Gandhi called for a campaign of civil disobedience. He also insisted that all protest be nonviolent. Gandhi said Thoreau was perhaps the greatest influence on how the struggle for India's independence was carried out. He called Thoreau "a great writer" and credited him as being "the chief cause for the abolition of slavery in America."

Years later (1950s and 1960s), in America, another great leader embraced the writings of Thoreau: Dr. Martin Luther King, Jr. Reverend King was determined to lead a civil rights movement that was nonviolent and based on Thoreau's ideas about civil disobedience.

Dr. King stayed true to his determination to protest without violence. Despite the many painful obstacles in his way—many of his followers were beaten, killed, or jailed—Dr. King did not waiver. King, too, was arrested numerous times for his role in the protests. While serving time in a jail in Birmingham, Alabama in 1963, Dr. King wrote a letter that expressed his commitment to civil disobedience.:

Martin Luther King, Jr. urged civil rights protestors to always march peacefully and respectfully.

One who breaks an unjust law must do so openly, lovingly, and with a willingness to accept the penalty. I submit that an individual who breaks a law that conscience tells him is unjust, and who willingly accepts the penalty of imprisonment in order to arouse the conscience of the community over its injustice, is in reality expressing the highest respect for the law.

chapter 3

Citizenship in Your Life

On a daily basis, citizenship is about getting involved. It's about participation. And it's about contributing something to a community larger than just your family or group of friends.

No matter what your age, there are lots of ways to get involved. School is one of the easiest places to become a good citizen. You can participate in school activities by voting in school elections, writing for the school paper, or contributing to school fundraising drives. What's more, you can also take a leadership role. You can run for a school office. Or you can become one of the managing editors of your school newspaper or yearbook.

School is one of the best places to practice good citizenship.

Good information helps you understand the world.

Getting Involved Means Getting Informed

An important step to becoming a good citizen is to be informed. You can't get involved in the world if you don't know what's going on in the world.

Information is everywhere. For example, you can find a great deal of news online. Newspapers and magazines are other great sources of news. Newspapers tend to give specific news about daily events. Magazines provide more general overviews of major issues that affect people all over the world. [See Resources on page 47.]

The Samantha Smith Story

The period between 1950 and 1989 is often referred to as the "Cold War era." During that time, the democratic United States was at odds with the communist Soviet Union (Russia and 14 other countries). In 1982, a ten-year-old girl named Samantha Smith became very concerned about the Cold War. She was frightened that the superpowers would destroy each other. The build-up of armies, military equipment, and nuclear weapons was especially scary.

Samantha wrote a letter to Yuri Andropov, the leader of the USSR. She asked Mr. Andropov directly if he intended to start a war. To her surprise, Mr. Andropov wrote back

Samantha Smith

to Samantha. He invited Samantha to come to the Soviet Union. He wanted her to see that they were peace loving and frightened by war, just like she was.

Samantha was so inspired by her trip that she decided to become an international spokesperson for peace. She traveled to Japan and many other places. She spoke to everyone about the need for peace.

In a tragic turn, Samantha was killed in a plane crash when she was only 13. She was flying back to Maine from a peace mission with her father.

Today, a life-sized bronze statue of Samantha stands outside the Maine State House in Augusta.

When you get informed, you learn about issues that become important to you. For example, you may read a story about deforestation (loss of trees) in the Amazon rainforest. The information you get may inspire you to do something about the problem. You may get more information from web sites and donate some money. Or you may volunteer some time or organize your own effort to help the cause. Your efforts can be small or large. You may, for example, educate the members of your family about ways to cut down on paper use in your home. On a larger scale, you may help to organize a program at your school to educate students, teachers, and administrators about paper-saving techniques, paper re-use, and recycling.

Making Choices and Getting Involved

Life is all about making choices. Deciding to become a person of good character is a choice.

Figuring out how to be a good citizen also involves choices. For example, voting involves choices: in order to cast a vote responsibly, you need to understand what you are voting for. That means, you need to be informed. And you need to have an idea of what the differences are between candidates or proposals.

Making your voice heard—especially by voting—is at the very core of citizenship.

Doris Haddock—known to millions as Granny D—did not let her age prevent her from getting involved.

Granny D

If you think someone can be too young or too old to make a difference, think again. And consider the story of Doris Haddock, known to millions as "Granny D."

Doris Haddock was born in New Hampshire in 1910. She spent most of her life living, working, and raising a family in New Hampshire.

John Muir "Citizen of the Universe"

Born in Scotland, John Muir came to America when he was 11 years old. Growing up on a farm in Wisconsin, John gained an appreciation for nature at an early age.

Roosevelt (left) with Muir

Later in life, Muir traveled to the Sierra Mountains of California. He was awed by the beauty of the wilderness known today as Yosemite. It was there that he realized his true calling was to inspire others to preserve the natural beauty of America. Muir called himself "a citizen of the universe" and felt it was everyone's duty to protect the wilderness.

By the late 1800s, Muir had become America's most famous and influential conservationist. In 1892, he founded the Sierra Club, which dedicated itself to the preservation of America's wild habitats.

After meeting Muir, President Theodore Roosevelt was inspired to create a wide range of conservation programs, including plans for establishing a national park system.

Muir used his influence to help create a number of national parks, including Yosemite, Mount Ranier, Petrified Forest, and Grand Canyon.

Today, John Muir is known as the "Father of America's National Parks."

Doris and her husband, Jim, were always involved in politics. They spent a good deal of their time fighting for causes in which they believed. In 1960, for example, the Haddocks helped to stop the planned use of hydrogen bombs in Alaska. Later in life, when she retired, Doris served on the planning board of her town and was active in other community affairs.

It wasn't until 1995 that Doris decided to get involved on a national level. She decided to fight for campaign reform—particularly to change the way candidates got money from supporters. Many people were concerned that donations to candidates were not regulated enough. Without regulation, candidates could accept large donations from supporters who,

At the age of 85, Granny D first began a national effort to change the ways campaigns are run. With her are Senator John McCain (left) and Senator Russell Feingold (pointing).

in turn, expect favors from the candidates once they are in office.

In January, 1999—at the age of 89—Doris began a 3,200 mile walk across America to raise support for campaign reform. Starting out in Los Angeles, California, she walked 10 miles each day for 14 months.

She traveled as a "pilgrim," which meant she walked until she was given shelter and she only ate when offered food.

Her incredible journey took her through 1,000 miles of desert, and through blizzard conditions in the Appalachian Range. It even forced her to ski for 100 miles when historic snowfall made walking impossible.

When she finally reached Washington, D.C. "Granny D" was greeted by more than 2,200 supporters. She was also met by several dozen members of Congress, all of whom walked the final few miles with her.

It took two more years of rallies and demonstrations in many states—and protesting around the Capitol in Washington—before Doris finally saw progress. The passage of the McCain/Feingold bill was the first step. This bill changed the way campaign contributions could be given and how they were documented.

Senator John McCain acknowledged the part Doris played in getting the bill passed. He also said of her, "She represents all that is good in America. She has taken up the struggle to clean up American politics...Granny D, you exceed any modest contributions those of us who have labored in the vineyards of reform have made....We are grateful to you."

After that victory, Granny D did not rest. She set her sights on other causes. In 2003, as a presidential election neared, Doris decided to work on raising awareness about voter registration. To do this, she drove around the country on a 22,000 mile voter registration effort. She especially targeted women and minorities. While on this journey in 2004, Doris heard some startling news. The candidate who was supposed to be the Democratic nominee for U.S. Senate in her home state of New Hampshire had dropped out of the race just days before the filing deadline. At the age of 94, Granny D surprised everyone when she announced that she would challenge the Republican candidate.

She vowed that her campaign would accept no large donations from special interests or big corporations. She wanted to run an honest campaign that focused on issues. She also wanted to show that politics was still open to "regular people" and not just to millionaires and incumbents (people already in office). And she had to do it all in less than four months.

By the time all the votes were counted, Granny D had made an astounding showing. She did not beat the incumbent, but she managed to capture 34% of the vote. This was a near miracle, given how little money her campaign spent and how little time she had before the election. Her impressive showing at the polls made it clear that many voters believed Granny D's cause was a just one.

Doris Haddock was determined to take part in changing America's political system. She did not let her age or any other obstacles stop her. For millions of Americans who have seen her or heard

Doris Haddock shakes hands with incumbent senator from Maine, Judd Gregg, during their live debate in 2004.

about her, Doris Haddock is a shining example of citizenship at its very best.

You can find out more about Granny D at grannyd.com. At the web site, there is also information about ordering the DVD documentary by Marlo Poras entitled "Run Granny Run" that aired on HBO.

Learning How to Make Good Choices

A famous lawyer and speechmaker named William Jennings Bryan once said, "Destiny is not a matter of chance, it is a matter of choice." He was saying that we have more control over our lives than we often assume.

More than anything else, your life will be affected by the choices you make. Knowing how to make good choices is most often the difference between being happy and being miserable.

Two Core Principles of Choice-Making

There are two fundamental principles that form the foundation of good decision-making. They are:

1. We all have the power to decide what we do and what we say.
2. We are morally responsible for the consequences of our choices.

The first principle goes back to what William Jennings Bryan said: your destiny is your choice. But what about when you feel powerless and out of control? We all feel this way at times—especially kids and teens.

Seeking good advice from people you trust is key to making sound decisions.

It's important to remember that having the power to make choices doesn't mean you have to make every choice alone. You also have the power to seek out good advice and to get the counsel of people you trust. So, part of making good choices is knowing how to get the help you need to make them.

The second principle is about understanding the full impact of the decisions you make. Every choice has a consequence—whether good or bad. And every choice affects certain people in some way. The people that are affected by a given choice are called "stakeholders." Most of us never even realize how many stakeholders there are for a given choice. Have you ever copied songs from a friend onto your MP3 player? Can you think of all the stakeholders affected by that choice? (Hint: It's not just you and the friend you copied from. Start thinking about the music download service, and the employees at the record company that sells the songs, and the musicians, producers, and engineers that work to create each song...).

So, thinking about all the stakeholders in a decision is one way to consider how important that decision is. It's another way of saying that the greater the consequence of a decision, the more important that decision is.

Okay, so now you know the principles of good decision-making. But the final part of the process is acting—actually making the ethical choice. Most of us know—most of the time—what the ethical choice is. The question is whether we *do it*—even if the consequences are costly to us or to others we care about.

Decision-Making Helpers

Choices are not always clear. Sometimes you will be pulled in many different directions as you consider what to do. Here are a few questions to ask yourself as you consider a decision. The answers may help to make the right choice clearer.

1. **Ask Yourself the Question of Universality**: If everyone made this choice, would it be a good thing?
2. **Ask Yourself the Golden Rule Question**: Would you want someone else to make this choice if it affected you the same way?
3. **Ask Yourself the Role Model Question**: Think of someone you know who is ethical and of strong character. What would that person do?

Building character is a lifelong process that takes courage, persistence, and strength.

Ethics Is Not for Wimps

Remember, being ethical is not always easy. It takes strength. And it often takes courage.

Being a person of strong character is not something that happens in a day or a week, or even years. For most "mere mortals," the strengthening of character is a lifelong process. There are always things to improve. Every year you work at it, your character will get better and better.

Ethical decisions can be difficult to make—and even more difficult to act upon. But great satisfaction and self-esteem come with knowing you did the right thing. Those positive feelings will inspire you to always make the right choices. This kind of satisfaction lasts a lifetime and brings you the most rewarding feeling of all: happiness.

Resources

WEB SITES:

CharacterCounts.org: The official site of CHARACTER COUNTS! provides information on programs, offers free resources and materials for students, parents, and teachers; also includes links to many other valuable and related sites.

TimeforKids.com; Newsweek.com; MSNBC.com; CNN.com: All reliable news web sites with information on today's headlines as well as stories on current issues from around the world.

Sierraclub.com: Official web site of the organization founded by John Muir. Get the newsletter, information on trips, learn about conservation, and other nature and wilderness issues.

Grannyd.com: Official web site about Doris Haddock, with information about her political career and links for related web sites, including how to order the DVD documentary "Run Granny Run," that aired on HBO.

NOTABLE BOOKS ABOUT CITIZENSHIP:

Who Was Martin Luther King, Jr.? by Bonnie Bader: published by Grosset & Dunlap, 2007.

The Adventures of Blue Avenger by Norma Howe: published by HarperTeen, 2000.

Let It Shine: Stories of Black Women Freedom Fighters by Andrea Pinkney: published by Scholastic, 2001.

My Side of the Mountain by Jean Craighead George: published by Puffin Books, 2004.

The Trumpet of the Swan by E.B. White: published by HarperTrophy, 2000.

Created Equal: Women Campaign for the Right to Vote by Ann Rossi: published by National Geographic Children's Books, 2005.

To Establish Justice: Citizenship and the Constitution by Patricia Mckissack and Arlene Zarembka; published by Knopf Books for Young Readers, 2004.

Glossary

Abolitionist: someone who worked to end slavery

Apathy: not caring about an outcome

Boycott: an organized refusal to buy a specific product or use a specific service

Civil disobedience: protesting without violence; while still respecting the law

Civic duty: action expected of a member of society

Civic virtues: actions that enhance society, such as running for elected office

Ethics: guidelines about right and wrong

Integrity: knowing and acting on what is right

Stakeholders: people affected by a decision

Suffrage: the right to vote

Universality: applied to everyone

Index

Photo Credits